D1015014

THE FRAGILE EARTH

EARTH · AT · RISK

THE FRAGILE EARTH

by Richard Amdur

Introduction by
Russell E. Train

Chairman of
the Board of Directors,
World Wildlife Fund and
The Conservation Foundation

CHELSEA HOUSE PUBLISHERS

new york   philadelphia

KRAXBERGER SCHOOL LIBRARY

CHELSEA HOUSE PUBLISHERS
EDITORIAL DIRECTOR: Richard Rennert
EXECUTIVE MANAGING EDITOR: Karyn Gullen Browne
EXECUTIVE EDITOR: Sean Dolan
COPY CHIEF: Robin James
PICTURE EDITOR: Adrian G. Allen
ART DIRECTOR: Robert Mitchell
MANUFACTURING DIRECTOR: Gerald Levine
PRODUCTION COORDINATOR: Marie Claire Cebrián-Ume

EARTH AT RISK
Senior Editor: Jake Goldberg

Staff for *The Fragile Earth*
EDITORIAL ASSISTANT: Mary B. Sisson
SENIOR DESIGNER: Marjorie Zaum
PICTURE RESEARCHER: Villette Harris
COVER ILLUSTRATOR: Yemi

Copyright © 1994 by Chelsea House Publishers, a division of
Main Line Book Co. All rights reserved. Printed and bound in the
United States of America.

 This book is printed on recycled paper.

First Printing

1 3 5 7 9 8 6 4 2

Library of Congress Cataloging-in-Publication Data
Amdur, Richard.
   The fragile Earth/Richard Amdur: introductory essay by Russell
E. Train.
      p. cm.—(Earth at risk)
   Includes bibliographical references and index.
   Summary: An examination of the earth's atmosphere and its
effects on living things.
   ISBN 0-7910-1572-6
         0-7910-1597-1 (pbk.)
   1. Earth—Juvenile literature. [1. Earth. 2. Atmosphere.]
I. Train, Russell E., 1920— . II. Title. III. Series.   93-827
QB631.4.A43 1993   CIP
363.7—dc20   AC

363.7
AMD

T 25049

C O N T E N T S

INTRODUCTION

Russell E. Train

Administrator, Environmental Protection Agency, 1973 to
1977; Chairman of the Board of Directors, World Wildlife
Fund and The Conservation Foundation

There is a growing realization that human activities increasingly
are threatening the health of the natural systems that make life possible
on this planet. Humankind has the power to alter nature fundamentally,
perhaps irreversibly.

This stark reality was dramatized in January 1989 when *Time*
magazine named Earth the "Planet of the Year." In the same year, the
Exxon *Valdez* disaster sparked public concern over the effects of human
activity on vulnerable ecosystems when a thick blanket of crude oil
coated the shores and wildlife of Prince William Sound in Alaska. And,
no doubt, the 20th anniversary celebration of Earth Day in April 1990
renewed broad public interest in environmental issues still further. It is
no accident then that many people are calling the years between 1990
and 2000 the "Decade of the Environment."

And this is not merely a case of media hype, for the 1990s will
truly be a time when the people of the planet Earth learn the meaning of
the phrase "everything is connected to everything else" in the natural
and man-made systems that sustain our lives. This will be a period when
more people will understand that burning a tree in Amazonia adversely
affects the global atmosphere just as much as the exhaust from the cars
that fill our streets and expressways.

Central to our understanding of environmental issues is the
need to recognize the complexity of the problems we face and the

relationships between environmental and other needs in our society. Global warming provides an instructive example. Controlling emissions of carbon dioxide, the principal greenhouse gas, will involve efforts to reduce the use of fossil fuels to generate electricity. Such a reduction will include energy conservation and the promotion of alternative energy sources, such as nuclear and solar power.

The automobile contributes significantly to the problem. We have the choice of switching to more energy-efficient autos and, in the longer run, of choosing alternative automotive power systems and relying more on mass transit. This will require different patterns of land use and development, patterns that are less transportation and energy intensive.

In agriculture, rice paddies and cattle are major sources of greenhouse gases. Recent experiments suggest that universally used nitrogen fertilizers may inhibit the ability of natural soil organisms to take up methane, thus contributing tremendously to the atmospheric loading of that gas—one of the major culprits in the global warming scenario.

As one explores the various parameters of today's pressing environmental challenges, it is possible to identify some areas where we have made some progress. We have taken important steps to control gross pollution over the past two decades. What I find particularly encouraging is the growing environmental consciousness and activism by today's youth. In many communities across the country, young people are working together to take their environmental awareness out of the classroom and apply it to everyday problems. Successful recycling and tree-planting projects have been launched as a result of these budding environmentalists who have committed themselves to a cleaner environment. Citizen action, activated by youthful enthusiasm, was largely responsible for the fast-food industry's switch from rainforest to domestic beef, for pledges from important companies in the tuna industry to use fishing techniques that would not harm dolphins, and for the recent announcement by the McDonald's Corporation to phase out polystyrene "clam shell" hamburger containers.

Despite these successes, much remains to be done if we are to make ours a truly healthy environment. Even a short list of persistent issues includes problems such as acid rain, ground-level ozone and smog, and airborne toxins; groundwater protection and nonpoint sources of pollution, such as runoff from farms and city streets; wetlands protection; hazardous waste dumps; and solid waste disposal, waste minimization, and recycling.

Similarly, there is an unfinished agenda in the natural resources area: effective implementation of newly adopted management plans for national forests; strengthening the wildlife refuge system; national park management, including addressing the growing pressure of development on lands surrounding the parks; implementation of the Endangered Species Act; wildlife trade problems, such as that involving elephant ivory; and ensuring adequate sustained funding for these efforts at all levels of government. All of these issues are before us today; most will continue in one form or another through the year 2000.

Each of these challenges to environmental quality and our health requires a response that recognizes the complex nature of the problem. Narrowly conceived solutions will not achieve lasting results. Often it seems that when we grab hold of one part of the environmental balloon, an unsightly and threatening bulge appears somewhere else.

The higher environmental issues arise on the national agenda, the more important it is that we are armed with the best possible knowledge of the economic costs of undertaking particular environmental programs and the costs associated with not undertaking them. Our society is not blessed with unlimited resources, and tough choices are going to have to be made. These should be informed choices.

All too often, environmental objectives are seen as at cross-purposes with other considerations vital to our society. Thus, environmental protection is often viewed as being in conflict with economic growth, with energy needs, with agricultural productions, and so on. The time has come when environmental considerations must be fully integrated into every nation's priorities.

One area that merits full legislative attention is energy efficiency. The United States is one of the least energy efficient of all the industrialized nations. Japan, for example, uses far less energy per unit of gross national product than the United States does. Of course, a country as large as the United States requires large amounts of energy for transportation. However, there is still a substantial amount of excess energy used, and this excess constitutes waste. More fuel-efficient autos and home heating systems would save millions of barrels of oil, or their equivalent, each year. And air pollutants, including greenhouse gases, could be significantly reduced by increased efficiency in industry.

I suspect that the environmental problem that comes closest to home for most of us is the problem of what to do with trash. All over the world, communities are wrestling with the problem of waste disposal. Landfill sites are rapidly filling to capacity. No one wants a trash and garbage dump near home. As William Ruckelshaus, former EPA administrator and now in the waste management business, puts it, "Everyone wants you to pick up the garbage and no one wants you to put it down!"

At the present time, solid waste programs emphasize the regulation of disposal, setting standards for landfills, and so forth. In the decade ahead, we must shift our emphasis from regulating waste disposal to an overall reduction in its volume. We must look at the entire waste stream, including product design and packaging. We must avoid creating waste in the first place. To the greatest extent possible, we should then recycle any waste that is produced. I believe that, while most of us enjoy our comfortable way of life and have no desire to change things, we also know in our hearts that our "disposable society" has allowed us to become pretty soft.

Land use is another domestic issue that might well attract legislative attention by the year 2000. All across the United States, communities are grappling with the problem of growth. All too often, growth imposes high costs on the environment—the pollution of aquifers; the destruction of wetlands; the crowding of shorelines; the loss of wildlife habitat; and the loss of those special places, such as a historic structure or area, that give a community a sense of identity. It is worth noting that growth is not only the product of economic development but of population movement. By the year 2010, for example, experts predict that 75% of all Americans will live within 50 miles of a coast.

It is important to keep in mind that we are all made vulnerable by environmental problems that cross international borders. Of course, the most critical global conservation problems are the destruction of tropical forests and the consequent loss of their biological capital. Some scientists have calculated extinction rates as high as 11 species per hour. All agree that the loss of species has never been greater than at the present time; not even the disappearance of the dinosaurs can compare to today's rate of extinction.

In addition to species extinctions, the loss of tropical forests may represent as much as 20% of the total carbon dioxide loadings to the atmosphere. Clearly, any international approach to the problem of global warming must include major efforts to stop the destruction of forests and to manage those that remain on a renewable basis. Debt for nature swaps, which the World Wildlife Fund has pioneered in Costa Rica, Ecuador, Madagascar, and the Philippines, provide a useful mechanism for promoting such conservation objectives.

Global environmental issues inevitably will become the principal focus in international relations. But the single overriding issue facing the world community today is how to achieve a sustainable balance between growing human populations and the earth's natural systems. If you travel as frequently as I do in the developing countries of Latin America, Africa, and Asia, it is hard to escape the reality that expanding human populations are seriously weakening the earth's resource base. Rampant deforestation, eroding soils, spreading deserts, loss of biological diversity, the destruction of fisheries, and polluted and degraded urban environments threaten to spread environmental impoverishment, particularly in the tropics, where human population growth is greatest.

It is important to recognize that environmental degradation and human poverty are closely linked. Impoverished people desperate for land on which to grow crops or graze cattle are destroying forests and overgrazing even more marginal land. These people become trapped in a vicious downward spiral. They have little choice but to continue to overexploit the weakened resources available to them. Continued abuse of these lands only diminishes their productivity. Throughout the developing world, alarming amounts of land rendered useless by over-grazing and poor agricultural practices have become virtual wastelands, yet human numbers continue to multiply in these areas.

From Bangladesh to Haiti, we are confronted with an increasing number of ecological basket cases. In the Philippines, a traditional focus of U.S. interest, environmental devastation is widespread as deforestation, soil erosion, and the destruction of coral reefs and fisheries combine with the highest population growth rate in Southeast Asia.

Controlling human population growth is the key factor in the environmental equation. World population is expected to at least double to about 11 billion before leveling off. Most of this growth will occur in the poorest nations of the developing world. I would hope that the United States will once again become a strong advocate of international efforts to promote family planning. Bringing human populations into a sustainable balance with their natural resource base must be a vital objective of U.S. foreign policy.

Foreign economic assistance, the program of the Agency for International Development (AID), can become a potentially powerful tool for arresting environmental deterioration in developing countries. People who profess to care about global environmental problems— the loss of biological diversity, the destruction of tropical forests, the greenhouse effect, the impoverishment of the marine environment, and so on—should be strong supporters of foreign aid planning and the principles of sustainable development urged by the World Commission on Environment and Development, the "Brundtland Commission."

If sustainability is to be the underlying element of overseas assistance programs, so too must it be a guiding principle in people's practices at home. Too often we think of sustainable development only in terms of the resources of other countries. We have much that we can and should be doing to promote long-term sustainability in our own resource management. The conflict over our own rainforests, the old growth forests of the Pacific Northwest, illustrates this point.

The decade ahead will be a time of great activity on the environmental front, both globally and domestically. I sincerely believe we will be tested as we have been only in times of war and during the Great Depression. We must set goals for the year 2000 that will challenge both the American people and the world community.

Despite the complexities ahead, I remain an optimist. I am confident that if we collectively commit ourselves to a clean, healthy environment we can surpass the achievements of the 1980s and meet the serious challenges that face us in the coming decades. I hope that today's students will recognize their significant role in and responsibility for bringing about change and will rise to the occasion to improve the quality of our global environment.

A photograph of the earth taken by astronauts on the Apollo 17 lunar landing mission. At the top of the photograph the Arabian peninsula is visible; at the bottom of the photograph is the Antarctic ice cap.

T H E   E A R T H   I N   S P A C E

By the late 20th century, human beings had launched
a great number of spacecraft, satellites, and unmanned probes
into the heavens. These machines of exploration have produced
a rich body of new knowledge in the form of rock samples from
the moon, close-up photographs of the rings surrounding Saturn,
Jupiter, Neptune, and Uranus, and tantalizing glimpses of bizarre,
distant objects at the edge of the known universe. In a relatively
short span of time, our knowledge of the universe and of the
earth's place within it has risen immeasurably.

In the ancient world, however, ideas about how the stars
and planets were related were radically different from our current
understanding. The earth was thought to be at the center of the
universe, with the sun, moon, planets, and distant stars revolving
around it. This idea was known as the Ptolemaic system, named
after the 2nd-century astronomer Ptolemy of Alexandria, and it
held sway well into the 16th century.

The Ptolemaic system was challenged by Nicolaus
Copernicus (1473–1543), a Polish astronomer who took the bold

step of removing the earth from its position at the center of the universe and claiming that the earth revolved around the sun. His heliocentric, or sun-centered, universe was denounced by the Catholic church as heresy. It seemed inconceivable to religious authorities that God would not place human beings at the center of things. But the subsequent work of such astronomers as Johannes Kepler (1571–1630) and Galileo (1564–1642) confirmed the Copernican vision, with some significant modifications.

The Copernican theory replaced the Ptolemaic theory because it could explain more simply and comprehensively the motions of the planets. With their model of the solar system in correct order, astronomers began to see the universe as a great machine set in motion by natural forces. The groundwork for this

The Andromeda galaxy, a spiral galaxy similar in size and shape to the Milky Way galaxy of which the earth is a part.

view was laid by the English scientist and mathematician Isaac Newton (1642–1727). His *Philosophiae naturalis principia mathematica* (Mathematical Principles of Natural Philosophy), published in 1687, successfully applied mathematical principles to the complicated behavior of celestial bodies. In so doing, Newton discovered the law of gravitation, a natural force of attraction between all material objects. His conception of a "mechanical" universe operating according to a single unifying principle represented a startling scientific advance.

THE BIG BANG

The notion of the universe as a kind of big clock or machine could explain how it might work but not how it came into being. Obviously, there must have been a time in the distant past when the universe was very different from what it is today. How did the stars and planets form in the first place? This is the question asked by cosmology, a branch of astronomy that studies the origin and evolution of the universe. Scientists now believe that about 20 billion years ago all the matter in the universe was packed into an extremely dense and tiny space at an unimaginably high temperature. This "cosmic egg" then exploded in what is known as the Big Bang, marking the beginning of the universe. In fact, the story of the Big Bang is still unfolding. The instant of the Big Bang itself may be long past, but its repercussions continue to be felt.

The Big Bang produced a fireball of titanic proportions with a temperature measuring in the billions of degrees. In the first milliseconds immediately following the blast, matter and energy burst outward in all directions, literally stretching space.

A globular cluster known to astronomers as NGC 6341.

As space expanded, the matter and energy released by the fireball cooled. As matter cooled, highly energetic subatomic particles slowed enough to interact with each other, filling the universe with the simplest elements of hydrogen and helium. Driven by gravity and by their own momentum, these gases began to accumulate, first into small pockets and then into larger clumps that gradually grew hotter and brighter and evolved into stars. Stars were formed in this manner throughout the universe, and large groups of stars—some numbering in the hundreds of billions—formed the largest structures in the universe, galaxies.

Galaxies tend to occur in groups known as clusters. One such cluster, called the local group, contains our own galaxy, the Milky Way, and the Andromeda galaxy, also known as M31, the 31st object in the classification system devised by the French astronomer Charles Messier (1730–1817). The Milky Way is a spiral galaxy; that is, if viewed from afar it would resemble a spiral. Other major galaxy types are globular clusters, elliptical galaxies, and barred spirals, which have bars of dust, gas, and stars running across the galaxy's center like the spokes of a wheel. Still other galaxies are irregular, with no definite form. Some clusters of galaxies contain thousands of galaxies, and there are roughly 100 billion galaxies in the universe.

Within the galaxies, stars continued to form, burn, explode, die, and re-form. In a remote corner of the Milky Way galaxy about 5 billion years ago, a single gaseous cloud began to contract under the force of gravity. In the process it became less amorphous in shape. Its interior temperature began to rise. At the center of the cloud, a hot, dense sphere of hydrogen gas held together by gravitation began to radiate. A star had formed. This star was the sun.

Smaller condensations of matter began to form within the gaseous cloud, slowly revolving around the sun. These were the protoplanets, whirling accumulations of gas that would, in time, give rise to the planets. The protoplanets grew in size and, through the force of their own gravitation, absorbed other matter in the cloud, including other protoplanets. In this way the number of protoplanets lessened. Finally, the solar system took its modern shape: spherical planets with their moons locked into orbit around a central sun, located some 30,000 light years away from the center of the Milky Way. There might be more than 1 billion sunlike stars with planetary systems in the Milky Way galaxy alone.

The theory of a universe expanding from an initial violent explosion is based on observation of the behavior of distant galaxies. The light from these galaxies is red-shifted, that is, it appears redder than one would expect, given what is known of the chemical composition of the burning gases that are giving off the light. Astronomers have compared this effect to the Doppler shift in sound waves when the object making the sound is moving away from the observer. The Austrian physicist Christian Doppler (1803–1853) noted that the sound of a train whistle changes pitch and is heard as a lower-pitched sound as the train moves away from the listener. Because light is also a wave, the Doppler effect also works with light. If a luminous body is approaching, the wavelength of its light will be shortened and will move toward the blue end of the color spectrum. If a luminous body is receding, the wavelength will be longer and shifted to the red end of the color spectrum. It was the American astronomer Edwin

This diagram by a NASA artist shows a comet spiralling in toward the sun past the planets of the inner solar system—Mars, Earth, Venus, and Mercury.

Hubble (1889–1953) who determined that the wavelengths of light from other galaxies all indicated a shift to the red.

Hubble concluded that the galaxies were receding, moving away from the Milky Way and from each other in all directions. The most obvious intepretation of this phenomenon was that the universe was expanding. The idea that this expansion originated from the massive explosion of a single, dense "cosmic egg" was the work, among others, of the Belgian astronomer Georges Lemaître (1894–1966) and the American physicist George Gamow (1904–1968).

Difficult questions arise if one accepts the idea of a Big Bang and an expanding universe. What came before the Big Bang? Scientists do not know. Will the universe expand indefinitely or will it contract again, producing yet another Big Bang and another universe? This, too, is unknown. Why did the Big Bang occur? The realms of religion and folklore have given full play to nonscientific explanations, but science, seeking verifiable evidence, has yet to weigh in with a definitive response.

PLANET EARTH

It is not known whether earthlike planets are common in the universe, but scientists are well aware that a great many accidental conditions had to turn out just right to produce a planet capable of sustaining life as we know it. First and foremost is the earth's orbital position in space. The earth is located at just the right distance from the sun so that it is neither too hot nor too cold to support life. The surface temperature of the planet Venus, which is closer to the sun, is more than 900 degrees Fahrenheit. Farther from the sun than Earth, the planet Mars experiences

Venus, shrouded by thick clouds of sulfuric acid, is closer to the sun than the earth and absorbs and retains too much heat to be suitable for life. With an atmosphere made up mostly of carbon dioxide, Venus suffers from a runaway greenhouse effect, and its surface temperature is too high (900° F) for water to remain liquid.

bitterly cold nights and winters. These temperature extremes are among the many reasons that the two planets are inhospitable to life. Had the earth, during its formation, settled into an orbit different from its present one, it is unlikely that living creatures would have evolved at all.

One of the main reasons why the earth's orbital position is so critical is that the heat received from the sun makes possible a planetary surface covered by liquid water. No other planet in the solar system has a liquid water surface. There can be no liquid water on Venus because the high surface temperatures would cause it to evaporate into space, and liquid water is impossible on Mars for the opposite reason—surface temperatures are too low—and because there is not enough atmospheric pressure to hold liquid water in place. But the earth's temperature and atmosphere are just right. More than 70% of the earth's surface is covered by water, and water is essential to life. Living tissues are made up mostly of water, and the physical and chemical characteristics of water make biological processes possible.

Mars is farther from the sun than the earth and lacks a sufficient atmosphere to retain heat. Though water may have flowed across its surface millions of years ago, it is now a cold, dry planet.

*Sir Isaac Newton
(1642–1727), the English
scientist and mathe-
matician who explained
the orbits of the planets
with his new theory of
gravitational attraction.*

The earth also possesses an atmosphere unlike any other
in the solar system. Held in place by the force of gravity, the
atmosphere's various layers, each of a different density, allow
heat and light to reach the surface while filtering out dangerous
radiation. If the earth were less massive, there would not have
been enough gravitational force to prevent the escape into space
of these atmospheric gases. The moon, for example, has a mass
that is only about one-eightieth that of the earth, and it has no
atmosphere. If the earth's mass was greater than it is, its gravity
would have created an atmosphere containing heavy

hydrocarbons and other gases not conducive to life. Jupiter is more than 300 times as massive as Earth and possesses such an atmosphere. Early in its geologic history, the earth's atmosphere contained methane, ammonia, and other hydrogen compounds, but primitive blue-green algae in the oceans converted this mixture to one of nitrogen and oxygen, and the earth's mass and gravity kept the new atmosphere stable.

The earth seems unique in so many respects that it was thought by some observers to have been created in an entirely different way from the other planets in the solar system. But dating methods based on the measurement of radioactive decay put the age of the earth at roughly 4.5 billion years, corresponding quite nicely with the age of the solar system as a whole. The sun, planets, asteroids, meteors, and other celestial bodies all appear to have been created from the same primeval gas cloud. In the beginning, the earth's environment was hardly suitable for life. Meteors bombarded the earth in a nearly constant shower. The atmosphere, as mentioned, contained very little oxygen and was instead comprised of toxic gases. In the absence of a protective ozone layer, the sun's ultraviolet rays reached the surface of the planet with their full force, breaking up the complex organic molecules necessary for life, except where they were protected in the oceans. Surface temperatures were very hot, electrical storms were frequent, and most of the planet's surface was molten—the result of constant, violent volcanic activity.

But gradually the environment was transformed. Over the course of hundreds of millions of years, the planet cooled down from the heat of its own creation. On the surface, a thin, hard crust began to form. Oceans and lakes began to appear—the

Galileo Galilei (1564–1642), the Italian astronomer who challenged prevailing views by claiming that the sun, not the earth, was the center of the solar system.

result of accumulations of condensed water vapor. Simple biological organisms appeared in the seas, changing the ratio of gases in the atmosphere through photosynthesis.

The point is that the conditions necessary to produce a planet capable of sustaining life are very complex, and the right combination of such conditions is a very fragile balance that could easily have been upset had things happened only slightly differently. The earth's environment, which seems to us so solid, stable, and relatively unchanging over the course of a lifetime, is in reality a purely accidental combination of circumstances that has occurred nowhere else in the solar system, and perhaps nowhere else in the universe.

A computer enhanced image of Jupiter. Visible in the lower right center of the picture is the famous Red Spot, an enormous storm that has been raging ever since astronomers first began to observe the planet. Jupiter, a gas giant, can be considered a failed star. Had it been somewhat more massive, gravitational forces would have initiated a fusion reaction in its core, and the solar system would have two stars.

Charles Darwin (1809–1882), the English naturalist who first suggested that modern species evolved from ancient ones, changing over time as they adapted to new environmental conditions.

chapter 2

L I F E   O N   E A R T H

The evolution of life on earth and of the ecological systems that support life reveal an equally accidental chain of events that could very easily have produced a completely different set of results. Scientists do not yet know exactly what happened at the moment when life began. They do, however, agree on a general scenario that starts with the formation of amino acids and other complex organic molecules in the atmosphere roughly 3.5 to 4 billion years ago, in geological terms very soon after the planet's formation. Rains washed these amino acids down into the newly forming oceans. There, protected from the destructive power of solar and cosmic radiation, these molecules were able to interact and form even more complex combinations.

At some point, a certain kind of molecule formed that used other molecules as building blocks to produce a copy of itself. This molecule soon became more prevalent than those that could not reproduce themselves. According to population expert Paul Ehrlich, when this happened, "The distinction between organisms and environment appeared; self could be separated from non-self; life had originated." These molecules did not "desire" to reproduce themselves; it was simply a result of the laws of chemical bonding. Nevertheless, once a molecule gained the ability to replicate itself by reshaping other substances in its environment, another biological process was set in motion: evolution by natural selection.

NATURAL SELECTION

All living and reproducing creatures, even at the molecular level, compete to obtain the food, organic materials, and energy resources they need from the environment. Those creatures better adapted to obtain what they need are more likely to survive, thrive, and reproduce. Individuals that are less efficient at obtaining what they need or in replicating themselves are more likely to die out. Evolutionary biologists describe this process with the phrase "survival of the fittest," though it must be understood that "fittest" does not mean strongest or most aggressive but simply best adapted to the conditions existing in a particular environment. In fact, for modern biologists, fitness is mostly a matter of reproduction. Those creatures with the best chance to survive are those who can produce the most "copies," or offspring, and protect them until this next generation is itself able to reproduce. They are not necessarily the strongest creatures, but those best able to exploit the resources surrounding themselves. Nature shows no mercy to those organisms that cannot adapt, and they are eliminated rather quickly.

The theory of natural selection was developed by the English naturalist Charles Darwin (1809–1882). Darwin was interested in the degree of variation in animal populations, both within species and from species to species. In 1831, he embarked aboard the HMS *Beagle* on a five-year government research expedition to the South American coast and the Galápagos Islands. His extensive analysis of the animal and plant specimens led to the publication, in 1859, of *On the Origin of Species by Means of Natural Selection, or the Preservation of Favoured Races in the Struggle for Life*. Darwin's ideas in *The Origin of Species* were attacked by churchpeople as antithetical to the Biblical account of creation, but his theory remains the basis for scientific thinking about the evolution of life on earth.

The basic mechanics of the process of natural selection can be seen in the case of the European peppered moth. Prior to

In this drawing an apatosaurus witnesses the agent of its own destruction, an asteroid or comet that will strike the earth with enough force to alter the world's climate.

the Industrial Revolution, this light-colored moth lived on trees covered with lichen, blending in with its surroundings. But over decades, soot from industrial emissions gradually killed the lichen and blackened the trees, making the light moths easier for predators to see. As time passed, their numbers dwindled. Meanwhile, darker members of the same species eluded capture and eventually came to dominate. The lighter-colored moths are now found only in areas where there is little industrial activity.

Evolution by natural selection is the way in which living organisms change and develop into different organisms. The process of developing into a new organism takes place slowly as small changes accumulate, the result of natural variation in populations, minute mutations in genetic codes, and the effects of environmental pressures that become apparent only over long periods of time. Most of the changes that species undergo are not beneficial for survival, and these mutations disappear as failed biological experiments. But a few such changes have enormous survival value and are often adopted by broad groups of living creatures. A particular pattern of locomotion or protective behavior toward young, immature offspring may be found among many different species.

Eventually, self-replicating molecules formed the first single-celled organisms, which were better able to maintain their structures and reproduce themselves. Soon there evolved multicellular organisms in which molecular structures took on specialized functions. These organisms needed energy and organic materials to survive, grow, and reproduce, and for a while they were able to feed on the organic molecules in the primordial oceans. But these materials soon grew scarce. This problem was solved when some microorganisms developed the ability to harness the energy of the sun.

PHOTOSYNTHESIS

Photosynthesis is the process by which the energy of sunlight is used by living organisms to convert organic materials directly into food and living tissue. The process arose when certain microorganisms evolved a green pigment known as chlorophyll that was capable of capturing sunlight. Foremost among these microorganisms were single-celled algae, also called cyanobacteria because of their bluish green, or cyan, coloring. Cyanobacteria absorbed sunlight and used it as energy to manufacture starches, sugars, and celluloses from water and carbon dioxide in the atmosphere. This was a revolutionary development, for organisms that could photosynthesize could now feed themselves, giving them a powerful advantage over cells that depended on finding food in their nearby environment. Because the only things needed were sunlight, water, and atmospheric gases, conditions were ripe for the proliferation of cyanobacteria, and they multiplied and spread throughout the oceans.

Photosynthesis splits water into its constituent parts, hydrogen and oxygen. The hydrogen becomes part of the food-making operation, but the oxygen is an unwanted by-product and is set free and released into the atmosphere. Before living organisms employed photosynthesis, the atmosphere contained very little oxygen. In fact, the presence of oxygen, which is a highly reactive and poisonous gas, might have inhibited the emergence of life by destroying the complex organic molecules in the atmosphere. The success of the cyanobacteria in solving one environmental crisis—using sunlight as a new source of energy—created another crisis: an overabundance of deadly oxygen. How would living creatures not accustomed to high levels of atmospheric oxygen survive?

Eventually, some microorganisms developed the ability to produce an enzyme—a type of protein that functions as a catalyst in biochemical reactions—that neutralized the oxygen. Organisms with this enzyme triumphed over those without it. Then came another evolutionary leap. The organisms that had grown adept at neutralizing oxygen learned how to use it to their benefit by turning it into energy, beginning a process known as respiration. These new, oxygen-based life-forms soon became dominant.

The rising levels of oxygen meant that the atmosphere was evolving, too. The most important aspect of this change was the creation, through the interaction of oxygen and the sun's ultraviolet radiation, of a type of oxygen known as ozone. By about 1 billion years ago, an ozone screen had formed in the upper atmosphere, a protective layer that absorbed and blocked the sun's ultraviolet rays but allowed other, less harmful components of its light to reach the surface of the earth. This removed ultraviolet radiation as a threat to life on the planet and made it possible for living creatures to move out of the oceans onto dry land. Furthermore, an oxygen-based metabolism proved more efficient at extracting large amounts of energy from food, and organisms were free to evolve more elaborate systems of locomotion and reproduction.

THE CAMBRIAN EXPLOSION

There followed a long period during which living organisms evolved into many new forms and spread into new habitats all across the earth. Scientists call this long stage of the earth's history, which began about 600 million years ago, the Cambrian explosion. (*Cambrian* comes from the Latin for "Welshmen"; ancient fossils found in Wales gave the period its name.) Where once the seas had been filled with mostly bacteria and algae, after the Cambrian explosion they came to be populated by a great variety of living forms—plants and seaweeds, sea urchins, worms, and jellyfish. At first, these were all soft-bodied creatures. The acidity of the oceans was too high for Precambrian ocean-dwellers to develop shells or skeletons. Gradually, however, with the erosion of the land into the sea, the water's composition became less acidic. This in turn caused the epidermis, or outer layer, of some sea creatures to undergo calcification, a hardening of soft tissue through the addition of calcium, turning that outer layer into a shell. When these creatures died, their remains were further calcified into fossils. More important, while the animals lived, the shells provided protection against predators and an enclosed environment in which more sophisticated inner organs—brains and muscles, for example—could develop. The Cambrian oceans were filled with shell-building corals and vast numbers of many-legged, crablike creatures known as trilobites. The procession toward truly complex forms of life had begun.

About 400 million years ago, plants started to take root on land, and the animals who fed on them were quick to follow.

Coral formations from the seas near New Guinea. As ancient seas lost their acidity, creatures such as these corals developed protective shells or exoskeletons by absorbing calcium from the water.

Among the first, scientists say, were snails, worms, and a variety of insects. In the oceans, with the appearance of vertebrate skeletons, fishes came to predominate. The first land vertebrates were the amphibians, creatures located on the evolutionary scale somewhere between fishes and reptiles. Amphibians can survive on land but need lots of moisture and must lay their eggs in an aquatic environment. Modern amphibians include frogs, toads, salamanders, and newts.

As land vegetation became more and more profuse, the amphibians evolved into creatures that did not need water in

A fossil of an archaeopteryx, a flying reptile and an ancestor of modern birds.

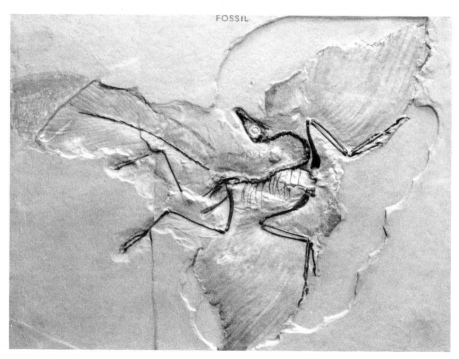

which to lay their eggs. These were the reptiles, among them tortoises, turtles, crocodiles, alligators, snakes, and lizards. They adapted more readily to the drier environment on the land and became the dominant life-form of the Mesozoic era, which lasted from 225 million years ago until 65 million years ago.

The most famous reptiles were, of course, the dinosaurs. They were the largest creatures ever to walk on land, and they reigned for most of the Mesozoic era, longer than the current "age of mammals" and many times as long as humans have existed. For many scientists, the true significance of the dinosaurs lies in the compelling mystery of their demise. What caused the extinction of the dinosaurs 65 million years ago and what does that tell us about the past, present, and future of the planet? Most experts agree that a dramatic change in the earth's climate must have occurred to which the dinosaurs and many other creatures could not adapt. They also agree that the change must have been of an unprecedented magnitude, because the dinosaurs had survived prior environmental calamities.

Controversy surrounds the issue of what prompted the catastrophe. Some say that it was a huge, sudden burst of radiation from the sun or from some other exploding celestial body. Others attribute it to a planetwide increase in volcanic activity or a shattering collision between the earth and a meteor or comet, both of which could have thrown up an enormous cloud of dust thick enough to block the sun's life-sustaining energy. Still others postulate the existence of a small, dim companion star orbiting the sun, which created havoc in the earth's environment when it passed nearby. Some scientists assert that the change in climate was not a single catastrophe at all but

Earthworms were among the first creatures, after the plants, to adapt to life on land.

an evolutionary process that happened over thousands of years and only appears abrupt because of the condensing effect of the geological scale of time.

Whatever the cause, the earth was wiped clean of these spectacular reptiles and millions of other species in what was clearly a random and unpredictable event. With the destruction of the great reptiles, habitats were emptied that could now be occupied by a new group of creatures—the mammals. Hairy, warm-blooded, and possessing a number of complex, specialized organs, including larger brains, mammals are now the dominant form of life on earth, but only because of a geological or cosmic accident. When dinosaurs ruled the earth, mammals were small in size and secretive in their habits. Their main problem was to avoid being eaten. With the dinosaurs gone, they were free to increase in size and numbers and to develop complex forms of social behavior that made them the hunters, not the hunted.

Except for a few unusual species, most modern mammals share a common ancestor—the shrew, a tiny, mouselike, tree-dwelling, insect-eating mammal. The shrews took to the trees to escape predation by dinosaurs and other reptiles. It is not known why they were able to survive the events surrounding the extinction of the reptiles, but they did. Within a few million years, they dramatically increased their numbers, left the trees for the ground, and evolved into a hugely varied array of successful mammal species. Among those mammals whose lineage can be traced to the tree shrew is *Homo sapiens.*

HUMAN ORIGINS

The scientist Carl Sagan once wrote, "Were the Earth to be started over again with all its physical features identical, it is extremely unlikely that anything closely resembling a human being would ever again emerge. There is a powerful random character to the evolutionary process. A cosmic ray striking a different gene, producing a different mutation, can have small consequences early but profound consequences late. Happenstance may play a powerful role in biology, as it does in history. The farther back the critical events occur, the more powerfully can they influence the present."

Most people can readily cite the most important characteristics that distinguish humans from other animals:

The tiny tree shrew was one of the few mammals small enough and stealthy enough to survive in the age of dinosaurs. All mammals, including human beings, are believed to have descended from the shrew.

upright posture, bipedal locomotion, and a large, specialized brain. Researching this transformation from the tiny tree shrew is the province of paleontologists, the scientists who study life in the past, as well as specialists in related disciplines such as paleobotany, paleoanthropology, and paleoclimatology. Relying on a sparse but revealing fossil record, these experts have pieced together a rough picture of how humans came into being.

The first primates in the evolutionary line following the tree shrews were the prosimians—lorises, lemurs, and tarsiers who lived from 40 to 70 million years ago. Mostly nocturnal tree-dwellers, the prosimians developed characteristics under the influence of arboreal life that later played a role in the emergence of human beings. The most important of these characteristics were grasping hands and stereoscopic vision.

Life in the trees required first and foremost an ability to hold on to limbs and branches. This brought about a change from

Reconstruction of the head of Cro-Magnon man, one of the immediate predecessors of modern Homo sapiens.

the clawed paw seen in the earliest prosimians to a hand with five articulated fingers. Over time, this would evolve into the opposable thumb, a distinguishing feature of humans that permits a precision grip capable of delicate tool manipulation. Some modern apes can achieve a less effective version of the precision grip, but because they are also adapted to knuckle walking on their forearms most apes and monkeys make do with a less refined grip.

Life in the trees also made demands upon the lower primates' eyesight. The need to see through the thick, tangled forest and to accurately judge the distance between branches resulted in larger, more powerful eyes, an increasing ability to see in color, and, most important, stereoscopic vision. Stereoscopic vision means that both eyes face forward, taking in a broad field of vision, and are able to focus simultaneously on a single object. The change from eyes located on either side of a long snout came about as the prosimians' sense of smell decreased in importance.

About 40 million years ago, the first apes and monkeys appeared. Modern monkeys are known as either Old World (residing in Africa and Asia) or New World (residing in Central or South America) monkeys. Unlike Old World monkeys, New World monkeys have different shaped noses and a grasping, or prehensile, tail that often serves as an extra hand. Larger than their prosimian predecessors, such monkeys as baboons and macaques are also more deft at moving through the trees. Prosimian locomotion tended toward leaping and clinging, but monkeys scamper along tree limbs on all fours, a skill known as arboreal quadrupedalism. The skeletal changes in the feet that accompanied this new method of locomotion were another evolutionary step toward human bipedalism.

The apes, a higher form of primate than the monkeys, are larger in size, do not have tails, and have bigger and more complex brains. The great apes include orangutans, gorillas, and chimpanzees; the lesser apes include gibbons and siamangs. Some of these apes developed a unique form of swinging known as brachiation as a means of moving through the forest. This required a more upright, humanlike posture. Swinging also provided a way of reaching fruit at the ends of limbs that probably eluded monkeys and prosimians. Jaws and teeth became smaller and craniums were growing to accommodate larger brains. Larger brain size was associated with the increasing use of hands and eyes.

But physical characteristics are not the only things linking humans with apes, monkeys, and prosimiams. Behavior, though different, displays some striking similarities. Like humans, apes use tools. The best-known example is of chimpanzees using twigs to fish edible termites out of their mounds. Both apes and monkeys live in social groups, with males more concerned with food-gathering and defending against predators. Most female primates form a close bond with their young and provide an extended period of nurturing through childhood, as do humans. Studies have also shown that many apes possess impressive problem-solving skills. Whether apes can master the use of language is a controversial issue. Apes in captivity have been taught sign language and have communicated simple needs and even emotions; however, they have yet to demonstrate an ability to string together sentences with true syntax.

Fossil analysis suggests that the first apes appeared about 30 million years ago. *Dryopithecus africanus* dates from the early Miocene epoch, about 15 to 20 million years ago, and may be a common ancestor of both modern apes and humans. Beyond the *Dryopithecines*, several important fossils point the way toward humans. *Gigantopithecus* was a large Miocene ape that lived from 6 to 9 million years ago. *Sivapithecus* was a smaller contemporary that lived from 9 to 12 million years ago. *Ramapithecus*, still smaller at three feet tall, lived from 8 to 14 million years ago. Apelike in appearance, *Ramapithecus* had humanlike teeth and other traits that led some scientists to believe that it was the first known hominid—the earliest human ancestor. *Ramapithecus* lived in a time of great environmental change. For millions of years, forests had blanketed the continents. But during the Miocene epoch, the forests were replaced by vast grasslands and savannahs filled with enormous herds of grazing mammals. The apes, so well adjusted to life in the forest, were forced to confront this new environment and risk life in the open. Among their adaptations to life on the ground was one of enormous importance—they stood up. Upright posture led to many other changes. Hands were now free to carry food, fashion tools, and engage in more creative activities. This tended to increase the size and sophistication of the brain. A higher point of vision enabled early hominids to see over tall grass in search of prey or predators. With the hands now responsible for carrying, tearing up, and preparing food, the mouth was free to evolve the capability of speech, a process that was also encouraged by changes in brain size. Bipedalism itself became more efficient the more it was used. These evolutionary developments supported each other and produced qualitative leaps in intellectual and social interaction within early human communities.

These adaptations, when viewed in terms of the progression toward modern humans, seem to represent logical

An artist's reconstruction of the head of a young Australopithecus africanus, *an ape with many human characteristics.*

steps. But in fact the course of evolution might have been radically different if the change in global climatic conditions that produced the grasslands had occurred at some other time—5 million years earlier or 5 million years later. With a slight variation in circumstances, a very different kind of ape, monkey, or prosimian might have emerged. The path toward *Homo sapiens* was fortuitous, not logical, an accident of timing in the course of evolutionary history.

No trace of *Ramapithecus*'s descendants has been found, owing to a gap in the fossil record of several million years' duration. But the pace of evolutionary change appears to have accelerated during this interval. When the fossil record begins again, 3 to 4 million years ago, several types of hominid are found, all of them tool-using, upright-walking meat-eaters covered with hair and standing about four to five feet tall. These were the ape-men known as australopithecines. Though they had some apelike traits—protruding jaws, and brains about the same size as the great apes—australopithecines were clearly in the line of human evolution.

Australopithecus africanus and its larger, stockier relative, *Australopithecus robustus*, are currently viewed as the direct ancestors of modern humans. Until the discovery of *Australopithecus afarensis* in 1974, *Australopithecus robustus* was viewed as a dead end and *Australopithecus africanus* was seen as the likeliest ancestor of modern humans. It now appears that *Australopithecus africanus* came before *Australopithecus robustus* and that the line became extinct approximately 1 million years ago. *Australopithecus afarensis* dates from 3.5 million years ago and is said by its discoverer, Dr. Donald Johanson, to be the hominid variety that preceded other species in the line that became modern humans.

The australopithecines were still alive during the ascendency of two new hominids—*Homo habilis* and *Homo erectus*. *Homo habilis*, the earliest member of the *Homo* genus, lived about 2 million years ago, stood about five feet tall, had a larger brain than the australopithecines, and is seen as a direct ancestor of *Homo erectus*.

Homo erectus lived from 1 to 1.5 million years ago. The species exhibited another increase in height and brain size and possessed limbs that indicate highly developed upright walking. This ancestor of modern humans is often called Peking man or Java man, the names coming from the sites of excavations in China and Indonesia. Both sites revealed extensive evidence of stone tool use, as well as the fossils of other animals such as rhinoceros, deer, and elephants. Paleontologists have concluded that *Homo erectus* knew how to make and use fire, probably skinned animals to make garments, and may even have been capable of language. Surprising as it may seem, *Homo erectus* may not have been all that different from modern hunter-gatherers. Even so, he was not yet a *Homo sapiens*.

Paleontologists are still trying to account for the jump between *Homo erectus* and *Homo sapiens*. One candidate seen as a possible link is *Homo sapiens neanderthalensis*, or Neanderthal man. Neanderthal remains date from 75,000 to 35,000 years ago and have been found throughout Europe. But the span of time between *Homo sapiens neanderthalensis* and *Homo sapiens* is thought to be too short to account for significant differences in height, brain size, and other features, and

Neanderthal man is now seen as a separate offshoot of the line
that led to modern humans.

THE WEB OF LIFE

Human beings may be the predominant form of life on
the planet, and the most powerful in terms of culture and
technology, but they do not live in isolation from other living
things. Humans are part of a complex, delicate, interdependent
web of life. This web contains millions of species of plants,
insects, fish, birds, amphibians, reptiles, and mammals, as well as
a wide range of unique ecosystems, from tropical rainforests to
temperate deciduous forests, from grasslands and savannahs to
desert scrub, and from alpine tundra to coastal marshlands.

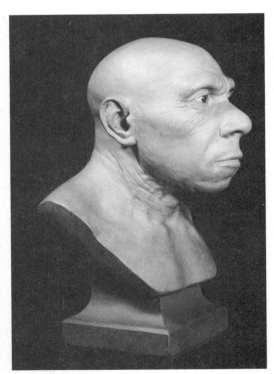

*A reconstruction of the head
of Neanderthal man, who
lived from 75,000 to 35,000
years ago.* Homo sapiens
neanderthalensis *is no longer
considered an ancestor of
modern humans, but a parallel
branch that became extinct.*

During the first half of the 20th century, the achievements of the Industrial Revolution led many people to believe that human beings were on the verge of conquering nature, of separating themselves from the web of life and surviving solely through the power of science and technology. If nature were to fail us in some way, there would always be a new chemical or process to rescue us from our dependency on the natural world. This has proven to be one of the greatest fallacies of modern times.

Scientists are just beginning to realize how little they know about the interrelationships between environments, living creatures, and human beings. As more and more of the natural environment is ravaged, the connections become more obvious. Human beings cannot survive without clean air and clean water. They may not be able to grow sufficient food if the earth experiences a significant warming. And they may not even be able to safely walk under the open sky if industrial chemicals destroy the earth's protective ozone layer. Changes to our environment may promote the growth of dangerous pests and disease organisms and destroy the predators that control them. The extinction of one species of phytoplankton or wild grass may permanently alter the food chain that human beings depend upon.

The interdependencies in nature are so complex, and the effects of changes so difficult to predict, that scientists are now suspicious of any effort to conquer nature and break the web of life. Protection and preservation of natural environments is now regarded as essential to human survival. The more one species dominates nature, biologists now believe, the closer that species may come to ensuring its own extinction.

KRAXBERGER SCHOOL LIBRARY

A bolt of lightning is a perfect symbol for the dynamic and chaotic physical processes at work on the earth.

chapter 3

EARTH DYNAMICS

It is useful to view the earth as consisting of four regions: the lithosphere, that part of the earth consisting of solid
rock; the hydrosphere, the planet's oceans and surface water;
the atmosphere, the gaseous envelope surrounding the earth; and
the biosphere, the relatively narrow zone extending a few miles
above and below sea level in which life occurs.

These regions interact in an intricate dynamic of
biological, chemical, and physical processes—some cyclical
and repetitive, others happening basically at random. Many of
these processes are essential to the continuation of life on the
planet. They regulate the earth's temperature and the strength of
solar radiation reaching the surface, the balance of atmospheric
gases, the availability of water, the creation and erosion of soils
that support agriculture, the competitive balance between
different species, and the alterations to ecosystems that direct
evolutionary change.

THE LITHOSPHERE

The lithosphere is divided into three concentric shells: the crust, mantle, and core. The core, extending from the planet's center out to a radius of about 2,000 miles, is divided into an inner core of dense iron and nickel and an outer core thought to consist of mostly molten iron. Surrounding the hot core is the mantle, which extends outward for another 1,800 miles and is divided into lower and upper parts composed of magnesium and iron silicates and other materials that serve as a sort of structural support for the earth's outermost layer, the crust.

The crust is a relatively thin covering with an average thickness of 20 miles that provides the planet with its continents and ocean basins. The continental material is mostly granite and is known as *sial* because it is rich in the elements silicon and aluminum. The oceanic material, and the material that underlies the continental sial, is largely basalt and is known as *sima* for being rich in silicon and magnesium. It would be a mistake to think of the crust, mantle, and core as a solid, immobile mass of rock and metal. Though changes to the lithosphere usually occur over long periods of time, it is continually evolving.

The earth's crust and upper mantle are broken into a number of slabs or "plates" of various sizes that sit atop a soft part of the lower mantle known as the asthenosphere. The shapes of these plates do not necessarily conform to the outlines of the continents. The Indo-Australian plate, for example, includes Australia, the South Asian subcontinent, and much of the Indian Ocean. The African plate encompasses not only the African continent but also much of the Arabian peninsula, part of the

Indian Ocean, and a part of the south Atlantic Ocean reaching almost as far as the east coast of Brazil.

Though they appear rigid, the earth's plates are in motion. They move away from each other, collide with each other, and grind against each other. The borders between plates where this grinding occurs are often the sites of frequent earthquakes and volcanic activity because of the tremendous heat and pressure generated by plate collision. The plates themselves are really the upper, cooler, more solid portions of huge convective currents of fluid rock, with hot, molten materials rising from the mantle, cooling to form new crust and then sinking again at the plate edges. These circular motions of heat and cold are common in the atmosphere and may be created within the earth's core and mantle because of heat generated by naturally occurring radioactivity. In this manner, over geologic time, the crust of the earth continually re-creates itself and generates new configurations of the planet's oceans and land masses. This action is known as *plate tectonics.*

The theory of plate tectonics is based on oceanographic research showing that sea floors spread as a result of the continual welling up from the mantle of hot, molten material known as magma. If the sea floors are spreading, the theory goes, some of the planet's ocean basins must be growing. This means that the continents must be moving apart from each other or closer to one another. There is much evidence to suggest that the shapes and positions of the earth's land masses were very different in past ages and that they will be different in the future. Plate movements happen at a rate of only a few centimeters per year, but over the course of millions of years the tiny increments add up to great changes.

Scientists now know, for instance, that the continents were once joined together as a single land mass, called Pangaea. About 200 million years ago, plate movements caused the break-up of Pangaea. The first phase of this process was its separation into two enormous continents, the northern one known as Laurasia, the southern one as Gondwanaland. By 65 million years ago, these supercontinents had become smaller bodies of land more closely resembling today's continents. This "continental drift" continues today. If the movement of the underlying plates persists at current rates, in about 50 million years the African plate will close in on the Eurasian plate, virtually eliminating the Mediterranean Sea, and the Pacific plate will have moved west enough to detach much of California and other areas west of the San Andreas Fault from the rest of North America.

This desert landscape in Haiti was once covered by forest. Destructive human activities can be just as effective as geophysical processes in rendering an area unsuitable for living creatures.

Plate tectonics provided answers to long-standing scientific speculation over remarkable similarites in the mountain ranges, flora, and fauna of continents divided by vast oceans, and to the puzzle over why the continents appeared to map-viewers as if they could be neatly fitted together like the pieces of a jigsaw puzzle. But tectonics also explains a wide range of geological and geophysical events, such as earthquakes, volcanoes, mountain-building, and more. Like Newton's theory of gravity, plate tectonics is a unifying theory.

Earthquakes usually occur along fault lines, places where two plates are sliding past each other or rubbing against each other. Volcanoes are often found underwater along mid-ocean ridges where two plates are moving apart and also on continental areas where two plates meet. Both phenomena involve the release of pressure built up over the long course of plate movements, which creates geothermal activity deep within the earth's core and mantle. Mountain ranges, such as the Himalayas and the Andes, and ocean trenches—such as the Mariana trench near the Philippines, which is deeper than any mountain on earth is high—are formed where plates converge and one plate is subducted, that is, slides under the other, causing a buildup of land formations. Converging plates also cause the gradual rise of the continents. The Tibetan Plateau, once located at sea level, is now some three miles above it.

THE HYDROSPHERE

The hydrosphere consists of all the water on earth and can be thought of as the liquid that fills in the spaces and gaps created by the lithosphere—the ocean basins, land depressions,

A plume of steam and volcanic ash rises from Mt. St. Helens in 1989. Such volcanic eruptions are evidence of violent changes taking place below the earth's surface, and the large quantities of dust that enter the atmosphere may alter the earth's climate.

catchment areas, gulleys, underground caves, and any other part of the earth's crust where water might collect. Slightly more than 97% of the planet's water is located in the oceans and seas. Approximately 2% is frozen in glaciers and polar ice caps, and the remaining 1% is found in rivers, lakes, and groundwater. All of this water continually circulates in what is known as the hydrological, or water, cycle.

The process by which water circulates begins with the large-scale evaporation of water over the oceans, which is caused by heat from the sun. As the water vapor rises, it is carried over land by air currents and there it falls to the ground in the form of rain or snow. Some of this precipitation runs off the land into streams and rivers and returns directly to the oceans. Some finds its way into underground aquifers, huge areas of porous rock that drain much more slowly. And some water is absorbed by the forests and vegetation, nourishing plant life. Water absorbed by plants is recirculated back into the atmosphere through a process known as transpiration as moisture evaporates from leaves. Water vapor carried from oceans to polar or high mountain land areas almost always falls as snow. This helps to build the ice caps and glaciers that characterize these regions. Here, too, water returns to the oceans as warmer weather causes chunks of glaciers and ice sheets to break off into icebergs.

The continuous circulation of the earth's water purifies it and makes it available to living creatures all over the land. As far as we know, life without liquid water is impossible. Without the proper recycling of water through the hydrosphere, life would not have evolved beyond the oceans.

THE ATMOSPHERE

The atmosphere is a kind of gaseous blanket draped over the hydrosphere and lithosphere, held in place by its own weight. Arrayed in discrete layers differing in temperature, pressure, density, and chemical composition, it has also been likened to an ocean, with human beings and the other life forms at the planet's surface occupying its very depths: the troposphere. The troposphere extends to roughly six or seven miles above the earth's surface and is the region in which most weather occurs. Above the troposphere is the stratosphere, which extends from about 6 to 30 miles above the surface. Above that is the mesosphere, which extends upward from about 30 to 50 miles. The thermosphere above the mesosphere extends from about 50 to 400 miles, and above that is the exosphere, which begins at 400 miles above the surface and has no definite upper limit, merging gradually with outer space.

Within those layers are other layers defined by their composition and the activity that takes place within them. The ozonosphere is found at about 60 miles above the planet's surface within the mesosphere. Here energy from the sun and from deep space is absorbed by molecules of ozone and prevented from bombarding the planet with lethal radiation. In the chemosphere, extending from 6 to 90 miles above the surface, photochemical reactions occur. The ionosphere above it encompasses the mesosphere and thermosphere and contains charged particles such as ions and electrons that reflect electromagnetic waves. Approximately 80% of the atmosphere, by mass, is in the troposphere, and nearly all of the atmosphere is within 20 miles of the earth's surface.

By volume, oxygen makes up just 21% of the atmosphere. Most of the atmosphere, roughly 78%, is made up of nitrogen. Argon (.9%), carbon dioxide (.03%), and traces of helium, neon, krypton, and xenon make up the remainder. In areas of dense human habitation, one can also find concentrations of chemicals and gases such as nitric acid, sulfur dioxide, and other artificial compounds. The greater the distance from the earth's surface, the lower the concentration or density of atmospheric gases. The atmosphere becomes progressively thinner. As one would expect, atmospheric pressure also decreases as altitude increases. Temperatures fluctuate with distance from the earth, at first decreasing to well below zero in the mesosphere and then increasing to several thousand degrees Fahrenheit above zero in the thermosphere.

Below the ozone layer, the natural mixture of gases absorbs heat, some directly from solar radiation but mostly from the earth. Some of this heat is eventually radiated into space, but a good deal of it is trapped by the atmosphere through the *greenhouse effect*, warming the atmosphere and helping to create and modulate the temperatures and conditions necessary for terrestrial life.

The atmosphere is always in motion, always trying to achieve thermal equilibrium by distributing its heat through the movement of air currents. These movements constitute the weather, and atmospheric changes occur much more rapidly than changes in the lithosphere or even the hydrosphere. Temperature differences are the natural result of the sun's uneven heating of the earth, and wind is the motion of air masses reacting to temperature differences and to local variations in atmospheric

More than 97% of the earth's water is found in the oceans. Through a complex cycle of evaporation and pre-cipitation, pure, salt-free water collects in lakes and rivers on the land and nourishes living creatures before return-ing to the sea.

pressure. Humidity, cloud formation, and precipitation are products of the atmosphere's interaction with the hydrosphere. Averaged out over time, these and other manifestations of weather make up *climate*, the characteristic weather of a given region.

Scientists have identified five general types of climate: moist equatorial and tropical climates, such as that found in the rainforests of Brazil, Indonesia, and central Africa; arid, dry, desert climates, such as that found in the Arabian Peninsula, Saharan Africa, most of Australia, and the American West; temperate climates, such as the climate of most of Europe and the United States east of the Rocky Mountains; colder temperate climates, as in much of Canada and the former Soviet Union; and polar climates, including the Arctic and Antarctic regions as well as the higher reaches of the Himalaya mountain ranges. These varying climates play an important role in dictating the kinds of life that occur in the earth's biosphere.

THE BIOSPHERE

The biosphere is not as rigidly defined as the earth's other spheres and in fact includes parts of the lithosphere, hydrosphere, and atmosphere. The biosphere is the zone of life, characterized more than anything else by its astonishing diversity. Life on earth can be found in a roughly ten-mile-thick belt extending from the ocean depths to the heights of the tallest mountains. Ecologists divide the biosphere into regions known as biomes, which are geographical areas with specific patterns of climate, vegetation, and other unique physical, chemical, and biological characteristics. Tropical rainforests are one type of biome; deserts, temperate forests, grasslands, tundras, and oceans are others. Within these biomes are countless, varied ecosystems that have achieved some kind of specific identity and biological stability. One of the most important elements in achieving biological stability within an ecosystem involves the creation of a dynamic balance between producers, consumers, and decomposers in what is known as a food chain.

The producers are the green plants, because they alone are capable of photosynthesis, of using the sun's energy to turn carbon dioxide and water into food for themselves. That food or energy is fixed within the plant in the form of chemical bonds. It is used by the primary consumers—herbivores such as insects, rodents, and cattle—who feed on green plants.

Secondary consumers—carnivores such as hawks, snakes, coyotes, lions, and humans—prey on herbivores. Finally there are the decomposers: the bacteria, dung beetles, and carrion-eaters such as vultures who feed on animal waste or the dead bodies of plants and animals. Decomposers cause dead creatures to decay, thereby breaking down chemicals and returning vital nutrients to the environment. The cycle of the food chain begins again when primary producers reuse these nutrients for their own sustenance.

Examples of sequences in a food chain include hawks feeding on rabbits who feed on desert grasses, and foxes feeding on rodents who feed on plant roots and seeds, and so on. Several primary consumers can feed on the same producers, and several secondary consumers can feed on the same primary consumers. The sum total of these connections is a food web. Food webs vary in complexity from biome to biome. A tropical rainforest hosts an amazing variety of species and an abundance of complex food webs, while a desert or polar region supports a relatively small

Tropical rainforests are the most biologically rich ecosystems on the planet. Though they occupy no more than 7% of the earth's surface, they support more than 50% of all living species.

number of species. In all cases, the interactions of species within the food web are themselves another set of conditions necessary for the existence of life. If, within a particular ecosystem or biome, there are not enough primary producers to feed the consumers, or if something disrupts the activities of the decomposers, that ecosystem is not stable and many species will die out.

Vital nutrients are continually recycled through the biosphere. One such cycle involves carbon, an essential element of life. Green plants absorb carbon dioxide from the atmosphere and during photosynthesis turn it into complex food compounds containing carbon, hydrogen, and oxygen known as carbohydrates. Carbon dioxide is returned to the atmosphere when plants burn during fires, when animals breathe, and when plants and animals decay. Vital elements such as oxygen, hydrogen, sulfur, phosphorus, and nitrogen also cycle through the biosphere. Nitrogen is used to form essential plant proteins that become animal proteins upon ingestion by animals. When animals and plants die, denitrifying bacteria return nitrogen to the atmosphere.

A variety of organisms have evolved that can ingest and transform these elements at various stages of their biochemical cycling. Remove a few essential organisms and the whole cycle and all the creatures that depend upon it may collapse.

Some ecologists talk about the influence of human beings on their environment in terms of the earth's technosphere, which they define as the region in which human technology has altered or affected the biosphere. There is no denying the dramatic effects that human technology has had on the earth's environment. In clearing out natural environments to make life comfortable for one species—human beings—a technology-driven modern society may have upset the so-called balance of nature. The great fear is that human beings have become too successful and may have taxed the limits of the biosphere to support them. Soil degradation, for example, caused by modern agricultural techniques, may make it difficult for future generations to feed a growing human population. Scientists and ecologists protest that they have only begun to understand the complex relationships in the natural world—how the living community of organisms sustains itself—and that we must know a lot more before we recklessly alter the biosphere permanently to achieve short-term gains.

Pollutants and exhaust gases from industrial activity not only cause respiratory problems for people but may promote global warming and massive climate change in the future.

THE EARTH UNDER ASSAULT

Many scientists now believe that human beings constitute the greatest threat to the survival of the earth and its multitude of living creatures. Since the beginning of the Industrial Revolution, people have engaged in what scientists and other experts commonly describe as a reckless, full-scale plundering of the planet and its resources. Virtually no part of the planet's fragile environment has escaped unscathed. If accidents and random events have characterized the evolution of life on earth, the opposite is true of what human beings have done to the planet. With great deliberateness, humans have altered the earth's environment, believing that they could master or improve upon nature.

GLOBAL WARMING

Global warming is caused by the buildup of certain gases that trap heat in the atmosphere. This is actually a naturally occurring phenomenon known as the greenhouse effect. Some amount of global warming is required to create the conditions necessary for terrestrial life. But modern society's long-standing reliance on fossil fuels—primarily oil, gas, and coal used by automobiles and industries—has caused scientists to wonder if global warming is now out of control.

The burning of fossil fuels releases heat-trapping greenhouse gases such as carbon dioxide, methane, nitrous oxide, and chlorofluorocarbons (CFCs) into the atmosphere. According to the World Resources Institute, average global temperatures have already risen 1 degree Fahrenheit in the past 100 years; a further climb of 3 to 9 degrees is predicted by the middle of the 21st century, meaning that the heat buildup is accelerating.

Global warming has potentially disastrous consequences. According to the National Academy of Sciences, it could cause the polar ice caps to begin melting, bringing a rise of 1.5 to 3.5 feet in sea levels that would threaten coastal cities around the world. Poor countries such as Bangladesh, Egypt, and Indonesia—much of whose populations live on or near water—are thought to be particularly vulnerable. Additional dangers from global warming include increased worldwide desertification, widespread crop failures, intensified global storm activity, unpredictable rainfall patterns alternating between extreme drought and heavy flooding, and increased incidence of human skin cancer. In North America, the grain belt of the United States could shift northward from the country's midsection, perhaps ending up in Canada. Some scientists reject these nightmare scenarios and claim that there is not enough evidence to state conclusively that human activities are to blame for global warming. They suggest that the rise in temperatures might be the result of normal climatic variation or natural, historical cycles of atmospheric warming and cooling.

Environmentalists fear that this scientific disagreement will play into the hands of those who oppose restrictions on fossil-fuel technology and greenhouse gas emissions, restrictions that environmentalists consider vital if global warming is to be brought under control. They seek commitments from industry and government to reduce emissions and to invest money in such alternative technologies as solar power.

OVERPOPULATION

The world's population explosion continues. Though the population growth rate has slowed in some of the largest countries, notably Brazil, China, India, and Indonesia, the rate of increase remains alarmingly high in such places as Kenya and Nigeria. Overall, forecasts predict the doubling of the earth's current population of 5.1 billion in the next 30 to 40 years, with 90% of the increase coming in the mostly poor, developing countries of Africa and Asia.

The effects of overpopulation on the earth's fragile environment are direct and easy to discern. Too many people means more forests cut down for farmland, fuelwood, and other products; more air pollution from automobile and factory emissions; more water pollution from untreated sewage and poisonous industrial effluents; more garbage and toxic waste; more pesticides; more overgrazing; more nuclear waste and radiation leaks; and more of everything else that contaminates the environment—including more of the same technologies, attitudes, and political conflicts that have produced the current crisis.

The population explosion is also a controversial issue. It is, of course, much more than an environmental problem, for it is

Chemical wastes and toxic substances, carelessly disposed of, may over-tax the ability of the earth's natural systems to absorb and neutralize life-threatening materials.

intertwined with the appalling poverty and hunger faced by the majority of the world's people. Some population specialists say that the environmental threat from overpopulation arises from an imbalance between the number of people and the planet's limited fuel and food resources. The earth is said to have a specific carrying capacity that has been exceeded, causing widespread poverty, hunger, and ecological damage. This viewpoint emphasizes birth control, education, and improved status for women as the most effective means for achieving population control and, in turn, easing stress on the environment.

But according to Barry Commoner, the well-known scientist and environmentalist, the greatest factor in environmental pollution, in both the industrialized and less developed countries, is dependence on environmentally unsound technologies. The industrialized countries of Europe and North America, with economies based on chemical manufacturing processes, chemical-intensive agriculture, fossil fuel–burning vehicles, toxic raw materials, and nuclear power, have contributed by far the most to the world's current environmental predicament. Unfortunately, the lesser-developed countries, in their urgency to improve the lot of their peoples, have set off down the same questionable path.

Commoner argues that all countries must adopt technologies, such as solar power and organic farming, that permit ecologically sound economic development. He also favors drastic measures to reduce poverty. Poverty compels citizens of poor countries to have more children to produce more wage earners, exacerbating overpopulation. Poverty induces less developed countries to import pollution-generating technologies, agrochemicals, pesticides, and even toxic waste in the name of development. Poverty, in the end, produces more poverty, perpetuating the problem and the environmental crisis. Commoner is among many who have begun to call for a massive transfer of funds to the less developed countries of the world, possibly in the form of colonial reparations, as a dramatic step toward securing the planet's future.

DEFORESTATION

Forests protect watersheds, provide animal habitats, improve air quality, sustain biodiversity, and serve as living laboratories for scientific and medical research. More than 25%

of the prescription drugs sold in the United States, including treatments for heart disease and cancer, contain active ingredients derived from forest plants. But the world's forests, particularly the tropical rainforests of Africa, Asia, and Latin America, are being destroyed with frightening speed.

According to the Rainforest Action Network, roughly 125,000 square miles of tropical rainforest—an area roughly the size of Germany—are cut, cleared, or burned every year. At this rate, nearly all of the planet's tropical rainforests will disappear within the next quarter century, with potentially catastrophic consequences. The burning of tropical forests also contributes to global warming and accounts for an estimated 10% to 30% of all carbon dioxide emissions into the atmosphere.

Why so much devastation, and why so fast? Agricultural development accounts for just under half of all tropical de-forestation, most of it "slash-and-burn" cultivation practiced in poor countries where a farmer clears a small plot of land, exploits it, and then moves on to another plot. The need to continually clear new plots is encouraged by the low productivity of rain-forest soils, which will cease producing crops after several years of planting. Overpopulation and unequal land distribution ag-gravate this process, because clearing rainforest land is frequently the only option left for the growing numbers of poor people in need of subsistence plots.

Commercial logging accounts for about 25% of tropical deforestation. Timber is the most lucrative rainforest resource because of the demand in the United States, Canada, western Europe, and Japan for housing materials, furniture, paper, and other products. But forests in the United States are also being felled. According to the Wilderness Society, more than 343,000 miles of logging roads—eight times the mileage of the entire interstate highway system—crisscross U.S. national forests in a timber program run by the U.S. Forest Service that loses money.

Tropical rainforests are also cleared for fuelwood, oil and gas exploration, mining, cattle ranching, road-building, dam construction, and other large development projects. The enormous debts owed to Western banks by less developed countries creates yet another incentive for them to capitalize on their valuable rainforest resources. A mere 5% of the world's tropical rainforests receive government protection.

TOXIC CHEMICALS AND TOXIC WASTE

Toxic chemicals are in many ways the foundation of modern society. Their use in the fields of agriculture, food processing, health and medicine, and manufacturing has

Pesticides protect our crops from insects, but after spraying they may enter the soil and the water, first accumulating in the bodies of marine organisms and then in the human beings who eat them.

improved life throughout the world. But that success has been achieved at great cost, for it has become clear that toxic chemicals and chemical-based technologies pose an extraordinary threat to public health and the environment.

Toxic chemicals have been at the heart of some of the greatest environmental disasters of our times. An accident at a pesticide manufacturing plant in Bhopal, India, left thousands dead and hundreds of thousands more condemned to lifelong eye and respiratory ailments and other afflictions. Improper disposal of toxic waste at Love Canal, New York, caused the emergency abandonment of an entire neighborhood, but only after an increase in miscarriages, birth defects, cancer, and nerve damage alerted an unsuspecting public to the danger in its midst. But Bhopal and Love Canal are only two of the best-known cases. More than 65,000 synthetic chemicals are in common use in the United States, with another 1,000 introduced each year. One government study revealed that the average American's body tissue contains traces of more than 200 industrial chemicals and pesticides capable of causing cancer or birth defects. According to the National Toxics Campaign, more than 700 contaminants have been found in the nation's water supply—poisons that can damage the reproductive system, the nervous system, the cardiovascular system, the brain, and such vital organs as the liver and kidneys. Occupational exposure to toxic chemicals causes from 100,000 to 400,000 deaths and disabilities every year. Pesticides continue to degrade the land and taint groundwater, and deadly DDT, though banned in many Western countries, continues to be exported to the less developed countries.

Hundreds of millions of tons of toxic waste are generated by American industry every year, but only 10% is handled safely.

The rest is released into the water and air or disposed of on land. The U.S. Department of Defense produces more toxic waste than the top five chemical companies combined. Current disposal technologies are considered inadequate. Landfills and injection wells leak, and incinerators pollute the air and produce toxic ash that requires disposal. From 10,000 to 30,000 toxic waste sites directly threaten public health and the environment. Radioactive waste from nuclear power and weapons plants remains hazardous for tens of thousands of years. Spending on military-related toxic and radioactive waste cleanup has been estimated at $400 billion, more than the Apollo, Gemini, and Mercury space programs combined.

Environmentalists want more stringent regulations, greater enforcement, more commitment to environmentally sound practices by the corporations and military who use and create toxic materials, and, ultimately, a shift away from chemical-based technologies.

AIR POLLUTION

The yellowy brown haze that hovers almost continuously over such cities as New York, Los Angeles, and Mexico City is probably the most overt, everyday evidence of civilization's assault on the environment. The primary cause of air pollution is well known: the burning of fossil fuels for transportation, home heating, and industry. Other contributing factors include fires, the spraying of crops with insecticides, and radiation from nuclear power and weapons plants.

The health risk from excessive amounts of ozone, sulfur dioxide, carbon monoxide, and nitrogen oxides in the atmosphere

Large dams such as this one on the Little Tennessee River in North Carolina provide cheap electric power, but they alter the flow of rivers, flood forests, disrupt the biological activities of fish and other organisms, and put a great strain on local ecosystems.

led to some of the U.S. government's earliest environmental legislation. The first Clean Air Act dates back to 1970, the beginning of the modern environmental movement. Despite a fair amount of official attention, however, a deadly problem remains. According to the Sierra Club, "More than half of the people in the United States live in areas where the act's health standards for breathable air still are not met." Furthermore, clean air legislation only covers a small percentage of the poisons released into the atmosphere.

In recent years, pollution problems of a more long-term nature have emerged. One such problem is acid rain, defined as rain, snow, sleet, fog, or dust that is abnormally acidic. Acid rain has damaged thousands of lakes, rivers, and forests in Europe and North America and is also a threat to crops. Some atmospheric acidity occurs naturally, but human activity since the Industrial Revolution has doubled the amount; in some parts of Europe and America's northeast, acidity levels have increased nine-fold. The problem is complicated because atmospheric pollutants often travel on prevailing wind currents, ending up hundreds and even thousands of miles from their point of origin. The only short-term solution is to reduce emission levels, which many countries have begun to do with improved smokestacks and lead-free gasoline. But critics contend that this isn't enough and point to alternative, nonpolluting energy sources and increased recycling and conservation as the only effective long-term solutions.

Perhaps the most serious long-term air pollution problem is the gradual depletion of the earth's protective ozone layer. This is caused by the effects of chlorofluorocarbons (CFCs). CFCs are man-made chemicals used as coolants in refrigerators and air conditioners, as solvents, and as the gas used to create foam insulation. But when they escape into the atmosphere and reach the stratosphere, they are broken down by the sun's ultraviolet radiation, and the chlorine in them destroys ozone. This action produces the increasingly larger holes in the ozone layer that have been detected most dramatically over Antarctica. CFCs also trap heat, contributing to global warming. Ninety countries have agreed to phase out CFC production by the year 2000.

Though the need for clean water is obvious, knowing this does not seem to have prompted many significant changes in human behavior toward the water cycle. Factories, power plants, and sewage treatment facilities continue to spew wastes into lakes, rivers, and streams incapable of handling the discharges. Oil spills and marine dumping of garbage and medical waste continue to foul the oceans.

Agrochemicals continue to leech their way into groundwater sources. Aquifers are also contaminated by leaks from toxic landfills and waste sites, underground gas storage tanks, septic tanks, and sewage lines. More than 40 million Americans drink water with an unacceptably high lead content, which threatens hundreds of thousands of people with brain damage, growth retardation, heart attacks, strokes, high blood pressure, nausea, and arm and leg pains.

Like air pollution, water pollution received relatively prompt government attention with the passage of the Clean Water Act in 1972. But the act's modest goals are far from being realized. Regulations and cleanup efforts have not kept up with the pace of pollution.

BIODIVERSITY

The process of extinction and species loss is a normal part of the cycle of life and death. *Homo sapiens* did not exist for most of the planet's history. The dinosaurs and countless other species existed for millions of years but are no longer. However, human activities have hastened the rate of species loss, causing serious consequences that scientists are just beginning to understand.

Estimates of the current rate of extinction of species vary. Some scientists believe that it is 100 species per day, a rate believed to be 1,000 times faster than that found in nature prior to the ascent of *Homo sapiens*. Other scientists believe that present rates of human-induced species loss will reduce the number of species by at least 25% sometime in the next 50 years. In 1986, nine prominent biologists, members of the U.S. National Academy of Science, said: "The species extinction crisis is a threat to civilization second only to the threat of thermonuclear war."

Some scientists question these forecasts. The disagreement stems in great part because no one knows just how many

A dust storm dangerously reduces visibility on a Wisconsin highway. The mechanized processes of modern agriculture have increased rates of topsoil erosion throughout the United States.

species there are on earth. Roughly 1.5 million species have been catalogued by taxonomists, but it is believed that the total number of species on the planet may range from 5 million to 30 million and perhaps as high as 50 or 100 million. Because so many species remain uncatalogued, it is difficult to build reliable mathematical models from which to draw conclusions.

But there is little doubt that all life on earth is linked in a great, interdependent web, making species loss at any rate an important issue for human survival. The main cause of species loss is tropical deforestation; though rainforests cover only 7% of the earth's surface, they provide habitats for 50% to 80% of the planet's species.

Deforestation, of course, is part of a larger habitat crisis confronting most living creatures. As human activities pollute the environment and encroach on land and water habitats, species loss occurs. Global warming also contributes to species loss because changes in the atmosphere directly affect sensitive plant life. Depletion of the ozone layer permits deadly ultraviolet radiation to reach the earth's lower atmosphere, with potentially damaging effects to living organisms.

WASTE

Modern society has been called, with good reason, the "throwaway society." From disposable diapers to plastic food packaging, virtually all the products of modern life yield the same end result: trash. For years trash was simply that—garbage to be set out on the sidewalk or at the end of the driveway, picked up by a private or municipal hauler and carted away for burial in a local landfill. But that option is no longer a solution.

Eighty percent of America's garbage is disposed of in landfills, but many of those landfills, especially in the major metropolitan areas of the east coast, are or soon will be full. Many landfills, full or otherwise, are hazards in themselves, leaching toxins down into groundwater sources. Sending excess refuse to other states, exporting it to poor African countries in need of cash, or dumping it illegally in the oceans have been some of the new responses to the landfill crisis, but they only make the problem worse and environmentalists have called for banning these practices.

Incinerators, which now account for 10% of America's garbage disposal, are seen by many as a preferable alternative. Incinerators are effective at reducing the volume of trash, but they are very expensive to build and, in spite of their sophisticated designs, they pollute the air. Incinerator ash disposal is also a problem, leading many to conclude that incinerators are only a halfway measure.

Recycling seems to be one of the most promising methods of reducing the flow of waste. The United States recycles just 10% of its garbage, but Western European countries recycle 30% and Japan is the leader at 50%. To many environmentalists, even recycling is not enough because it represents yet another effort at controlling pollution after it has been created instead of preventing it in the first place. Environmentalists want pressure brought against industry to change its production technologies. Even then, it appears, some trash will always remain. Additional suggestions for refuse handling include higher garbage collection fees for individual households, stiff fines for improper disposal, and tax incentives for corporations to offer more efficiently packaged materials.

NUCLEAR POWER
AND NUCLEAR WASTE

Global warming caused by the burning of fossil fuels has given new life to the long-running argument in favor of nuclear power as a "clean" energy alternative. For the moment, however, the nuclear power industry is still reeling from the effects of major accidents and from persistent, well-founded public doubt about the safety of nuclear energy. In the former Soviet Union, the accident at the Chernobyl nuclear reactor in 1986 left millions living on irradiated land and created an ongoing public health emergency. In the United States, the accident at the Three Mile Island reactor in Pennsylvania in 1979 and recent revelations of

Farmers in Indonesia build terraces on the hillsides to hold water for rice cultivation and to reduce soil erosion.

monumental safety and waste disposal problems at the nation's aging nuclear weapons factories have hindered attempts at new nuclear power plant construction. Safety concerns about the Shoreham, New York, nuclear power plant, built at a cost of several billion dollars, led to a decision in 1991 to begin dismantling the facility before it generated a single watt of electricity. Advocates of nuclear power point to France, which relies on nuclear energy for the vast majority of its electricity, as an example of an industrialized country with a safe and successful nuclear program.

Reactor safety and radioactive waste disposal are the primary obstacles to the widespread use of nuclear power. Experts have yet to figure out a safe way of treating or disposing of radioactive waste. Deep burial is the most common method. France has developed a promising process known as vitrification that involves cooling and mixing nuclear wastes with molten glass before burial. Some of the waste produced by nuclear weapons plants, however, is a volatile radioactive mixture for which there are no known disposal techniques. New reactor designs said to reduce or eliminate the possiblity of a meltdown—the overheating of the nuclear core and consequent release of radioactivity—are now being tested.

POLITICAL CONFLICT

Linked in the interdependent web of life, human beings have an obvious, common interest in maintaining the health of the planet's environment. But in spite of the general awareness of the problem, divisive debate surrounds most environmental issues.

Environmentalists contend that corporations and businesses are not committed to safeguarding the environment because the expense would cut into profits. The business community responds that it is already spending millions to comply with environmental laws and to develop nonpolluting technologies, and that overzealous regulation would lead to bankruptcies, unemployment, and a decline in everyone's standard of living.

Environmentalists also charge that governments have failed to create and enforce appropriate legislation and that they lack the political courage to take certain controversial steps, such as cutting the military budget or exerting more influence over corporate decision-making. Environmentalists also worry about the complacency of the general public and its reluctance to reject short-term convenience in the interest of long-term environmental protection. The public has shown increasing willingness to take such actions as recycling and buying "green" or "environmentally friendly" consumer products. But the public has not shown as much support at the ballot box for environmental referendums or for candidates stressing environmental issues. Environmentalists fear that the public will not do more until environmental problems affect them much more directly in their day-to-day lives.

Environmental protection also involves serious conflicts between the industrialized and the less developed countries. The poor countries of the world aspire to Western standards of living, but to achieve this goal quickly will only intensify such problems as global warming and depletion of the ozone layer. Developed countries that have already polluted their environments now seem to want to dictate to less developed countries just how much economic growth they are entitled to. This has angered many developing countries. Why, they ask, should they be denied the fruits of economic progress? Why should they place environmental concerns ahead of growth when the industrialized countries never did? How can rich countries, in which 30% of the world's population uses 70% of the planet's resources, blame the poor countries when the rich countries are the primary culprits? Experts say there is plenty of blame to go around and that people should focus instead on a cooperative global effort to halt environmental degradation.

An artist's conception of a large asteroid striking the earth in prehistoric times. Such a collision may have thrown up a huge dust cloud around the globe, cooled the earth, and led to the extinction of the dinosaurs.

chapter   5

T H E   F A T E
O F   T H E   E A R T H

Approximately 5 to 15 billion years from now, the sun
is expected to exhaust its supply of hydrogen gas, the fuel that
feeds its internal nuclear fires. When that happens, the sun will
undergo a violent expansion to roughly 400 times its present size,
becoming what solar physicists call a red giant. This swollen, fiery
orb will engulf Mercury and Venus and blast the earth with
enough heat to set the oceans aboil and incinerate all life on the
planet. The earth will become an inert sphere of dead, celestial
rock. The sun, meanwhile, will eventually collapse again under
the force of gravity, becoming first a white dwarf and then a black
dwarf, smaller than it is now and incapable of giving off heat or
light. A unique chapter in cosmological history will have come
to an end.

T H E   D E A T H   S T A R

Long before the sun gives out, a different kind of
astronomical event could threaten the earth with an episode of
mass extinction similar to that which may have killed off the

KRAXBERGER SCHOOL LIBRARY

dinosaurs 65 million years ago. Many scientists suspect that the dinosaurs perished as a result of a collision between the earth and debris from outer space—perhaps a large falling meteor, asteroid, or comet. This is a controversial idea because it puts forward a cosmic catastrophe as the engine of change, challenging the long-held view of Darwinian evolution as a smooth, gradual process. The theory holds that the earth will likely experience another cataclysmic collision with an astral body.

Some scientists have further developed this idea by examining evidence in the fossil record showing that "great dyings" happen approximately every 20 to 30 million years, implying the existence of a clocklike, extraterrestrial mechanism guiding the fate of the earth. This was such an unexpected and improbable finding that the scientists who discovered it tried, unsuccessfully, to explain it away as a fluke or statistical anomaly. But some astrophysicists then suggested that the sun, like many stars in the universe, might be part of a binary star system with an orbiting "dark" twin, or companion star—dark because it is small, not very bright, and usually too far off in space to be detected.

Every 20 to 30 million years, it is thought, this companion comes close enough to its twin to disrupt the belt of asteroids orbiting the sun, sending some of them on a collision course toward the earth. The evidence of impact craters that one would expect to discover is limited because they tend to be eroded and filled in as a result of the planet's geological activity. Still, analysis of what impact craters there are lends credence to the theory, for they have been found at 20-million-year intervals. Even more startling, the cycle of their appearance coincides with that of mass extinctions.

The so-called death star was named Nemesis, after the Greek goddess of retribution. Its existence is by no means widely accepted. Many scientists say that earth-driven environmental changes are more likely to have caused mass extinctions and that mass extinctions are more gradual than sudden in character. Nonetheless, speculation continues, and the next visit by Nemesis, if it exists, is expected roughly 13 million years from now.

NUCLEAR SUICIDE

The end of the earth as we know it could also happen in the few minutes required for nuclear weapons to rain destruction upon the planet. Cities burned to the ground; billions of people and countless other life-forms killed by radiation poisoning; land contaminated for generations by radioactive fallout—these are some of the certain environmental consequences of nuclear war.

An artist's conception of what might happen to the surface of the earth and the cities upon it if there is a large increase in solar radiation resulting from the eventual expansion of the sun into a red giant.

The possibilities also include the onset of a nuclear winter in which soot and smoke from bomb-related fires shroud the earth in thick clouds for months or years, robbing land and sea life of sunlight. Limited numbers of human survivors, their immune systems compromised, would emerge from their shelters in a state of unimaginable psychological shock to confront a postnuclear world of death and disease in which the worst is yet to come. With ten thousand years of technology wiped out in an instant, the survivors would have little choice but to live like scavengers or the primitive hunter-gatherers of the Stone Age.

This scenario might sound somewhat obsolete in the current era of lessened tensions between the United States and the former Soviet Union. Yet enormous stockpiles of nuclear weapons remain in place. In addition, the unstable economic, political, and military situation in the new Commonwealth of Independent States has created considerable worldwide concern about present and future control over Russia's nuclear trigger.

In any case, nuclear proliferation was never an issue for the two superpowers alone. The nuclear club also includes France, Great Britain, China, and a number of other countries. Some nations have renounced the use of nuclear power for military purposes; others have not. International agreements have tried to impose a degree of security on nuclear arsenals. However, arms experts say that these pacts are no guarantee against nuclear weapons falling into the hands of terrorists or such renegade nations as Iraq or Libya who tend to flout the international order.

Even the continued use of nuclear power for civilian purposes is thought to raise the danger of nuclear weapons proliferation, because the technology and the raw materials can be obtained by various means, legal and illegal. Thus the threat of a devastating nuclear explosion—from a single, accidental blast to a deliberate, full-scale wartime escalation—cannot be discounted. Indeed, because today's weapons have thousands of times the destructive power of the bombs that destroyed the Japanese cities of Hiroshima and Nagasaki at the end of World War II, the nuclear threat is very much alive.

DEATH BY ENVIRONMENTAL DEGRADATION

One need not contemplate such extreme catastrophes in order to envision the end of life on earth. Humans are doing exceedingly well with their everyday activities in steering the planet toward a tragic death by environmental degradation. Global warming, overpopulation, deforestation, toxic waste, water pollution, acid rain, depletion of the ozone layer, the waste crisis—all of these problems are the direct results of human activities.

How much longer can the planet endure environmentally destructive activities? Scientists encounter great difficulties in trying to determine, based on current practices and trends, the earth's future environmental profile. A lack of sufficient information in critical areas, disagreement over the meaning of available data, and the uncertainties involved in predicting such large-scale trends are just some of the difficulties that inhibit the creation of reliable forecasts. Still, enough is known about global warming, deforestation, population dynamics, and other problems

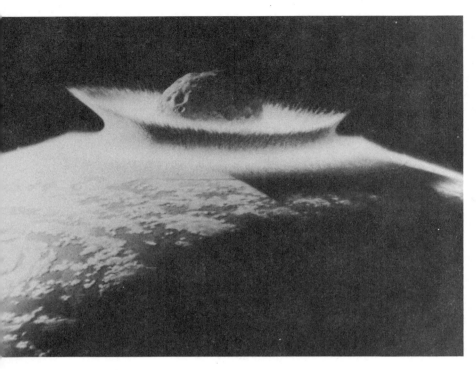

This painting by a NASA artist depicts a collision between the earth and an asteroid. In the past, when the solar system was still forming, such collisions were probably common, as evidenced by the cratered surface of the moon.

to make some projections. These generally envision an environmental catastrophe and economic and social collapse some time in the 21st century, perhaps in as little as 50 years, unless suitable action is taken beforehand.

Is there enough time to avert a calamity? According to the Worldwatch Institute, the 1990s is the decisive decade in which action must be taken. But the Worldwatch Institute is pessimistic about the earth's prospects. Worldwatch notes that since the

United Nations first focused global attention on environmental issues at its 1972 Conference on the Human Environment in Stockholm, the world has "not succeeded in turning around a single major trend in environmental degradation." Many commentators dismiss this gloomy prediction. Optimists claim that with human ingenuity, new technology, and global cooperation, disaster can be avoided.

If the optimists are right, what, then, is the proper response to the environmental crisis? Scientists, environmentalists, governments, corporations, and the public have varying, often conflicting notions of what is necessary and what is possible. Most people regard energy and resource conservation as an area where concrete steps can be taken without delay. At present rates of consumption, some of the earth's resources—timber, soil, metals, and many minerals—will likely last only a generation or two longer. Even the vast resources of coal, oil, and natural gas will be exhausted at some point, or become increasingly difficult and expensive to extract. This might actually be a blessing, because it would increase the attractiveness of alternative energy sources such as solar, wind, and wave power, which would become more economically competitive than they are at present.

The immediate benefit of energy and resource conservation would be to reduce the rate of degradation of air, land, and water environments. Pollution would also be reduced if the rate of consumption of resources is slowed. Pollution can only be controlled through the increased use of nonpolluting technologies in the fields of transportation, agriculture, manufacturing, and power production. Such technologies exist, but they are expensive.

Edwin Hubble at the Schmidt telescope on Mt. Wilson in California. Hubble studied the light from distant galaxies and concluded that the universe was expanding.

It may be necessary to redefine "economic growth," which has traditionally meant the ever-increasing production and consumption of new products. "Sustainable growth" is a new economic concept that seeks to regulate the production of goods and services so that human society does not take from the earth more than it returns. "National security" is another concept in need of updating. Traditionally it has meant large military budgets that constrain efforts to manage society's nonmilitary needs. The definition must be broadened to include adequate education, public health care, and urban aid.

Most issues come down to money at some point, and the environment is no exception. Slashing military budgets and the worldwide arms trade would free up vast resources for environmental cleanups and pollution prevention programs, and this seems a good, although politically sensitive, place to start finding the required funds. The crippling foreign debts faced by most of the developing nations must be forgiven by the banks and lending agencies, so that poor countries can use their limited cash resources to raise living standards. Wealth and resources must somehow make their way from the world's richest countries to the poor ones in a global effort to defeat poverty. A direct transfer of wealth is also politically unlikely, but aid programs such as the U.S.–sponsored Marshall Plan that helped rebuild Europe after World War II have been mentioned as starting points.

Perhaps just as important as money is forceful political leadership and an educated, involved, voting public willing to make the environment a make-or-break campaign issue. This task is largely for the industrialized countries, because they are mostly democracies and are responsible for most of the environmental

An aerial view of Cornell University's large radio telescope at Arecibo, Puerto Rico. The receiving dish is built into a depression between mountains, and the focal point for the radio waves is an observing station suspended above the dish from three pylons.

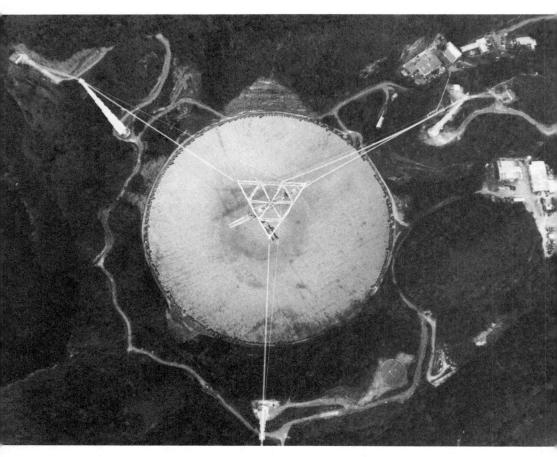

damage. The public must be informed about the life-styles changes and sacrifices that will be necessary. Corporations must prove that they care about the environment, and they should be required to grant greater public access to their decision-making processes on matters affecting the environment. Legislators must enact more effective laws and introduce taxes and financial incentives that steer corporations toward environmentally sound behavior. Presidents and prime ministers must rouse their people and seek multilateral cooperation through regional alliances and such global organizations as the United Nations. If this sounds like an environmental revolution, it is. The fragility of the earth and its ecosystems demands nothing less.

Appendix

FOR MORE INFORMATION

Citizens Clearinghouse for
  Hazardous Wastes
P.O. Box 926
Arlington, VA 22216
(703) 276-7070

Clean Water Fund
317 Pennsylvania Avenue SE
  (third floor)
Washington, DC 20003
(202) 547-2312

Environmental Action
  Foundation
1525 New Hampshire Avenue
  NW
Washington, DC 20036
(202) 745-4870

Environmental Defense Fund
257 Park Avenue South
New York, NY 20010
(212) 505-2100
(800) 225-5333

The Environmental Federation of
  America
3007 Tilden Street NW
Suite 4L
Washington, DC 20008
(800) 673-8111

Friends of the Earth
218 D Street SE
Washington, DC 20003
(202) 544-2600

Greenpeace USA
1436 U Street NW
Washington, DC 20009
(202) 462-1177

The National Audubon Society
950 Third Avenue
New York, NY 10022
(212) 832-3200

The National Parks and
  Conservation Association
1015 31st Street NW
Washington, DC 20007
(202) 944-8530

The National Toxics Campaign
29 Temple Place
Boston, MA 02111
(617) 482-1477

The National Wildlife
  Federation
1400 16th Street NW
Washington, DC 20036
(202) 797-6800

Natural Resources Defense
  Council
40 West 20th Street
New York, NY 10011
(212) 727-2700

The Nature Conservancy
1815 North Lynn Street
Arlington, VA 22209
(703) 841-5300

The Rain Forest Action Network
300 Broadway
Suite 28
San Francisco, CA 94133
(415) 398-4404

The Sierra Club
730 Polk Street
San Francisco, CA 94109
(415) 776-2211

The Union of Concerned
  Scientists
26 Church Street
Cambridge, MA 02238
(617) 547-5552

The Wilderness Society
1400 Eye Street NW
Washington, DC 20005
(202) 842-3400

The World Wildlife Fund
1250 24th Street NW
Washington, DC 20037
(202) 293-4800

F U R T H E R   R E A D I N G

Commoner, Barry. *Making Peace with the Planet*. New York: Pantheon, 1990.

Earthworks Group, The. *50 More Things You Can Do To Save the Earth*. Berkeley, CA: Earthworks Press, 1991.

————. *50 Simple Things Kids Can Do To Save the Earth*. Berkeley, CA: Earthworks Press, 1990.

————. *50 Simple Things You Can Do To Save the Earth*. Berkeley, CA: Earthworks Press, 1989.

Ehrlich, Anne H., and Paul R. Ehrlich. *Earth*. New York: Franklin Watts, 1987.

Ehrlich, Paul R. *The Machinery of Nature*. New York: Simon & Schuster, 1986.

Johanson, Donald C., and Maitland A. Edey. *Lucy: The Beginnings of Humankind*. New York: Simon & Schuster, 1981.

Leakey, Richard E., and Roger Lewin. *Origins*. New York: Dutton, 1977.

McKibben, Bill. *The End of Nature*. New York: Random House, 1989.

Raup, David M. *The Nemesis Affair: A Story of the Death of Dinosaurs and the Ways of Science*. New York: Norton, 1986.

Sagan, Carl. *Cosmos*. New York: Random House, 1980.

Schumacher, E. F. *Small Is Beautiful: Economics as if People Mattered*. New York: Harper & Row, 1973.

Weiner, Jonathan. *Planet Earth*. New York: Bantam Books, 1986.

GLOSSARY

acid rain Rain that has an abnormally high concentration of sulfuric and nitric acids; caused by industrial air pollution and automobile exhaust.

biodiversity The genetic variety in living species; the more species that exist, the greater the degree of biodiversity.

biome A region of the earth with a distinctive climate and vegetation.

biosphere All life that inhabits the earth—described as a biosphere because living things effectively surround the planet much as the atmosphere does.

bipedalism The ability to walk on two feet with upright posture.

conservation Planned management of a natural resource to prevent exploitation, destruction, or neglect.

deforestation The process of clearing forests.

ecosystem A community of living organisms and its environment functioning as an ecological unit in nature.

evolution The modification of species over time as a result of random changes, and the extinction of organisms less adapted to environmental conditions.

food web   The sum total of food chains linking producers, consumers, and decomposers.

global warming   The buildup of greenhouse gases in the atmosphere that is increasing the temperature of the earth's climate.

greenhouse effect   The trapping of infrared radiation in the earth's atmosphere by gases such as carbon dioxide and methane, which results in increased temperatures.

groundwater   Water beneath the earth's surface that flows slowly between soil and rock and supplies wells and springs; held in underground reservoirs called aquifers.

habitat   The place or type of site where a plant or animal naturally or normally lives and grows.

hydrosphere   The aqueous envelope of the earth, including bodies of water and aqueous vapor in the atmosphere.

landfill   A system of trash and garbage disposal in which the waste is buried between layers of earth and other substances such as clay.

lithosphere   The solid or rock-containing part of the earth.

natural selection   The process by which evolving organisms flourish or die because of their success or failure in adapting to the natural world.

nuclear energy   Energy released by splitting or fusing atomic nuclei.

overgrazing   Consumption of rangeland grass by grazing animals to the point that the grass cannot be renewed because of damage to the root system.

ozone layer   The invisible layer of gas that shields the earth's surface against dangerous ultraviolet radiation from the sun.

petrochemical   A chemical that is derived from petroleum or
   natural gas.

photosynthesis   The process by which plants convert sunlight into
   carbohydrates.

rainforest   A tropical woodland with an annual rainfall of at least 100
   inches and marked by lofty, broad-leaved evergreen trees forming a
   continuous canopy; also called a tropical rainforest.

watershed   A ridge or stretch of highland dividing the area drained by
   different rivers or river systems.

INDEX

Acid rain, 73, 87
Africa, 58, 65
"Age of Mammals," 36
Agrochemicals, 74
Air currents, 57
Air pollution, 65, 71–73, 77
Amino acids, 27
Amphibians, 35, 46
Andromeda galaxy (M31), 16
Antarctic, 58
Apes, 40, 41, 42, 44
Aquifers, 55, 74
Arabian Peninsula, 58
Arboreal quadrupedalism, 41
Argon, 56
Asteroids, 23, 84
Asthenosphere, 50
Atmosphere, 49, 55–58, 60, 61, 63
    chemosphere, 56
    exosphere, 56
    ionosphere, 56
    mesosphere, 56

    ozonosphere, 56
    stratosphere, 55
    thermosphere, 56, 57
    troposphere, 55, 56
Australia, 58
Australopithecines, 44, 45
Australopithecus afarensis, 44
Australopithecus africanus, 44
Australopithecus robustus, 44

Baboons, 41
Bhopal, India, 70
Big bang theory, 15–19
Biodiversity, 67, 74–76
Biomes, 58, 59, 60
Biosphere, 49, 58–61
Blue-green algae, 23, 31. *See also*
    Cyanobacteria
Brachiation, 41
Brazil, 58, 65

Calcification, 33
Cambrian explosion, 33–38

C o n v e r s i o n   T a b l e

(From U.S./English system units to metric system units)

Length

1 inch = 2.54 centimeters
1 foot = 0.305 meters
1 yard = 0.91 meters
1 statute mile = 1.6 kilometers (km.)

Area

1 square yard = 0.84 square meters
1 acre = 0.405 hectares
1 square mile = 2.59 square km.

Liquid Measure

1 fluid ounce = 0.03 liters
1 pint (U.S.) = 0.47 liters
1 quart (U.S.) = 0.95 liters
1 gallon (U.S.) = 3.78 liters

Weight and Mass

1 ounce = 28.35 grams
1 pound = 0.45 kilograms
1 ton = 0.91 metric tons

Temperature

1 degree Fahrenheit = 0.56 degrees
 Celsius or centigrade, but to
 convert from actual Fahrenheit
 scale measurements to Celsius,
 subtract 32 from the Fahrenheit
 reading, multiply the result by 5,
 and then divide by 9. For example,
 to convert 212° F to Celsius:

$$212 - 32 = 180 \times 5 = 900 \div 9 = 100° \text{ C}$$

PICTURE CREDITS

The Bettmann Archive: pp. 22, 60; Cornell University Photography/Chris Hildreth: p. 92; Courtesy Department of Library Services, American Museum of Natural History: pp. 24 (neg. no. 412423, photo C. Chesek), 29 (neg. no. 322113, photo Boltin), 34 (neg. no. 337963, photo Captain Frank Hurley), 35 (neg. no. 125065, photo Rota), 37 (neg. no. 125656, photo Logan), 39 (neg. no. 26178), 40 (left) (neg. no. 274667, photo H. S. Rice), 40 (right) (neg. no. 274668, photo H. S. Rice), 43 (neg. no. 313484), 46 (neg. no. 319951, photo Alex J. Rota), 48 (neg. no. 319948, photo R. E. Logan), 82 (neg. no. 322441, photo L. Boltin), 85 (neg. no. 320536, photo Boltin), 90 (neg. no. 2A2361); Luther Goldman/U.S. Fish and Wildlife Service: p. 66; Dr. P. James/University of Toledo, and NASA: p. 21; Library of Congress: p. 26; Lick Observatory, © UC Regents, University of California: p. 16; © Buddy Mays/Travel Stock: p. 78; NASA: pp. 12, 18, 20, 25, 88; National Oceanographic and Atmospheric Administration: p. 57; Palomar Observatory/California Institute of Technology: p. 14; Maggie Steber: p. 52; UPI/Bettmann: p. 54; U.S. Department of Agriculture: p. 69; U.S. Fish and Wildlife Service: p. 62; Wisconsin Department of Natural Resources: p. 75.

A B O U T   T H E   A U T H O R

RICHARD AMDUR is the author of *Toxic Materials* and *Wilderness Preservation*, also part of the Chelsea House EARTH AT RISK series. He has written *Anne Frank* in the CHELSEA HOUSE LIBRARY OF BIOGRAPHY series and three books in the Chelsea House WORLD LEADERS—PAST & PRESENT series: *Menachem Begin*, *Moshe Dayan*, and *Chaim Weizmann*. His articles have appeared in the *New York Times*, *Cosmopolitan*, and other periodicals. He lives with his wife in Brooklyn, New York.

A B O U T   T H E   E D I T O R

RUSSELL E. TRAIN, currently chairman of the board of directors of the World Wildlife Fund and The Conservation Foundation, has had a long and distinguished career of government service under three presidents. In 1957 President Eisenhower appointed him a judge of the United States Tax Court. He served Lyndon Johnson on the National Water Commission. Under Richard Nixon he became under secretary of the Interior and, in 1970, first chairman of the Council on Environmental Quality. From 1973 to 1977 he served as administrator of the Environmental Protection Agency. Train is also a trustee or director of the African Wildlife Foundation; the Alliance to Save Energy; the American Conservation Association; Citizens for Ocean Law; Clean Sites, Inc.; the Elizabeth Haub Foundation; the King Mahendra Trust for Nature Conservation (Nepal); Resources for the Future; the Rockefeller Brothers Fund; the Scientists' Institute for Public Information; the World Resources Institute; and Union Carbide and Applied Energy Services, Inc. Train is a graduate of Princeton and Columbia Universities, a veteran of World War II, and currently resides in the District of Columbia.